Cambridge **Discovery Education**™
▶ **INTERACTIVE READERS**

Series editor: Bob Hastings

SWING, SLITHER, SWIM

A2

Theo Walker

CAMBRIDGE
UNIVERSITY PRESS

Discovery
EDUCATION™

CAMBRIDGE UNIVERSITY PRESS
Cambridge, New York, Melbourne, Madrid, Cape Town,
Singapore, São Paulo, Delhi, Mexico City

Cambridge University Press
32 Avenue of the Americas, New York, NY 10013-2473, USA

www.cambridge.org
Information on this title: www.cambridge.org/9781107692428

First published 2014

Printed in Hong Kong, China, by Golden Cup Printing Company Limited

A catalog record for this publication is available from the British Library.

Library of Congress Cataloging-in-Publication Data

Walker, Theo.
  Swing, slither, swim / Theo Walker.
      pages cm. -- (Cambridge discovery interactive readers)
  ISBN 978-1-107-69242-8 (pbk. : alk. paper)
  1. Animals--Juvenile literature. 2. English language--Textbooks for foreign readers. 3. Readers
(Elementary) I. Title.

QL49.W198 2014
591.5'7--dc23

                                    2013014262

ISBN 978-1-107-69242-8

Additional resources for this publication at www.cambridge.org

Layout services, art direction, book design, and photo research: Q2ABillSMITH GROUP
Editorial services: Hyphen S.A.
Audio production: CityVox, New York
Video production: Q2ABillSMITH GROUP

Contents

Before You Read:
Get Ready!

Locomotion is the way things move and travel. Animals move in many different ways, and there are different names to describe these special kinds of locomotion.

Words to Know

Look at the pictures. Match the animals to their type of locomotion.

1. _____   2. _____   3. _____   4. _____   5. _____

flying squirrel   grasshopper   monkey   pangolin   snake

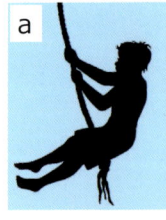
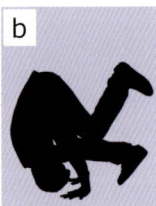

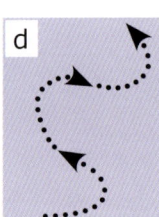

swing   roll   glide   slither   hop

Words to Know

Read the paragraph. Then label the parts of the animals with the correct highlighted words.

People have arms and legs and so do some animals. But animals sometimes have other names for these parts. The arms of fish and dolphins are called fins. Dolphins use their fins and tail to swim. The arms of birds are called wings. Eagles use their wings to fly down to their food and their claws to catch it. The penguin is a bird, but it cannot fly. It walks and swims. Its arms have a special name. They are called flippers.

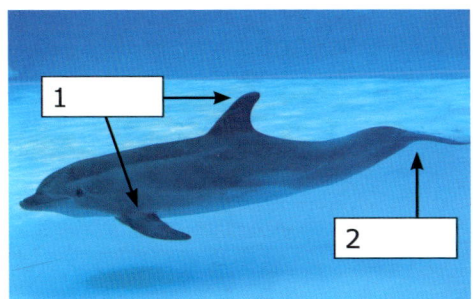

dolphin

penguin

eagle

?

ANALYZE

How are swimming and flying the same? How are they different? Explain your answer.

CHAPTER 1

How Many Ways Do Animals Move?

ANIMALS MOVE TO FIND FOOD AND STAY SAFE. SOME ANIMALS USE THEIR LEGS; SOME USE THEIR ARMS; AND SOME USE THEIR WHOLE BODIES TO MOVE. THERE ARE MANY KINDS OF ANIMAL LOCOMOTION.

A penguin

A centipede

A fish

Many animals move on two or more legs. A penguin walks on two legs. A horse runs on four legs. A grasshopper **hops** on six legs. A centipede walks on many small legs, and it can even run if there is danger.

Animals can also move quickly with their arms. A monkey uses its arms to climb trees and look for food. Birds use their **wings** to fly. Fish can swim thanks to their **fins**.

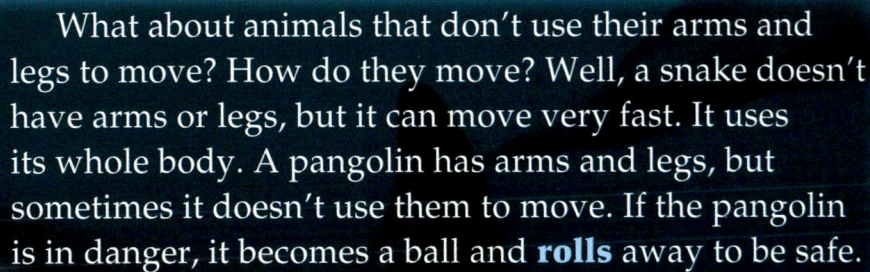

What about animals that don't use their arms and legs to move? How do they move? Well, a snake doesn't have arms or legs, but it can move very fast. It uses its whole body. A pangolin has arms and legs, but sometimes it doesn't use them to move. If the pangolin is in danger, it becomes a ball and **rolls** away to be safe.

Isn't it amazing how many kinds of **locomotion** there are? Each kind of animal has its own special way of moving.

? ANALYZE

Which animals move like people? Which animals move differently than people? What parts of their bodies do these animals use to move?

CHAPTER 2

Legs

NATURE SAYS "MOVE IT OR LOSE IT!" BUT LOSE WHAT? YOUR LIFE!

Animals often have to move fast to get away from danger. If they can run fast, they can get away and be safe. Is it better to have four legs or two when you want to run away from danger?

Horses run with four legs and they can run very fast. However, their legs are very slim, and they break easily. Also, horses get most of the sleep that they need standing up. So if a horse breaks its leg, this makes it very difficult for the leg to get better.

Penguins have two legs, but they can't run fast. In one hour, penguins can only walk about three kilometers across the ice of Antarctica. Penguins are birds, but they can't fly! But luckily for penguins, they can swim very well to get away from danger. Like ducks, penguins have wide feet. This helps them swim fast. Some penguins can swim at a speed[1] of 24 kilometers an hour!

Ostriches are the largest and heaviest birds in the world. Like penguins, ostriches cannot fly, but they can walk and run fast. In fact, they can run as fast as 70 kilometers an hour. Ostriches' legs are the longest of all birds, and they are very strong. Believe it or not, an ostrich can kill a person with one kick!

[1]**speed:** how fast something goes

?

ANALYZE

Horses have four legs that help them move fast. Can you think of other fast animals with four legs?

An ostrich running

Kangaroos also have powerful[2] legs. Their big back feet and long back legs are much larger and more powerful than their front feet and legs. This means that kangaroos can travel very fast, but they don't run. They hop. Kangaroos usually hop at speeds of 25–48 kilometers an hour.

Grasshoppers, like all insects, have six legs. They use their powerful back legs to hop very far. A grasshopper that is 2.5 centimeters long can hop 50 centimeters: That's twenty times its size! So, the grasshopper can move away from danger quickly. Grasshoppers also use their legs to make music! This tells other grasshoppers that danger is near.

[2]**powerful:** strong

Grasshoppers have powerful back legs.

Centipedes have even more legs than insects do. The word *centipede* means "one hundred feet," but some centipedes have only thirty feet, whereas others have three hundred! Their many legs help them move away from danger. Millipedes have more legs than centipedes,

A centipede

but millipedes move slowly because they have short legs that can't go very far. Centipedes also have two larger, special legs that they use to catch and eat their food – like teeth!

All of the animals in this chapter use their legs for locomotion. Some animals have more legs than others, but more does not always mean better. Each animal has its special way of moving to be safe.

leaf

branch

CHAPTER 3

Arms

DO YOU LIKE TO CLIMB TREES? DO YOU LIKE TO SWIM? ANIMALS USE THEIR ARMS TO CLIMB TREES, TO SWIM, AND ALSO TO FLY IN THE AIR. SOME ANIMALS USE THEIR ARMS TO CATCH FOOD AND TO **FIGHT**.

Koalas have strong arms and sharp[3] claws to climb trees where they eat and sleep. They eat the leaves that grow on the branches, and they sleep high up in the branches during the day where they are safe. Koalas can climb trees that are 30 to 60 meters high.

Monkeys also need to have strong arms to climb trees. Monkeys live in trees, and they get a lot of their food there. Monkeys like to eat lots of different things, but mostly they eat leaves and fruit. Monkeys can use their tails like another arm. That helps them climb to get different kinds of food to eat.

[3] **sharp:** something sharp can cut like a knife

Monkeys can move away from danger very quickly in the forest by **swinging** between branches. They hold the branches with their hands or tails and swing their bodies from tree to tree. Monkeys' hands are so strong that they can hold branches with only one finger!

Like other animals, penguins use their powerful flippers to swim fast towards food and away from danger. But penguins also use their flippers to fight. When penguins cannot move to safety in time, they hit other animals with their hard flippers to make them go away.

Video Quest

Orangutans

Watch this video to learn about the arms of orangutans. What can orangutans do that people cannot?

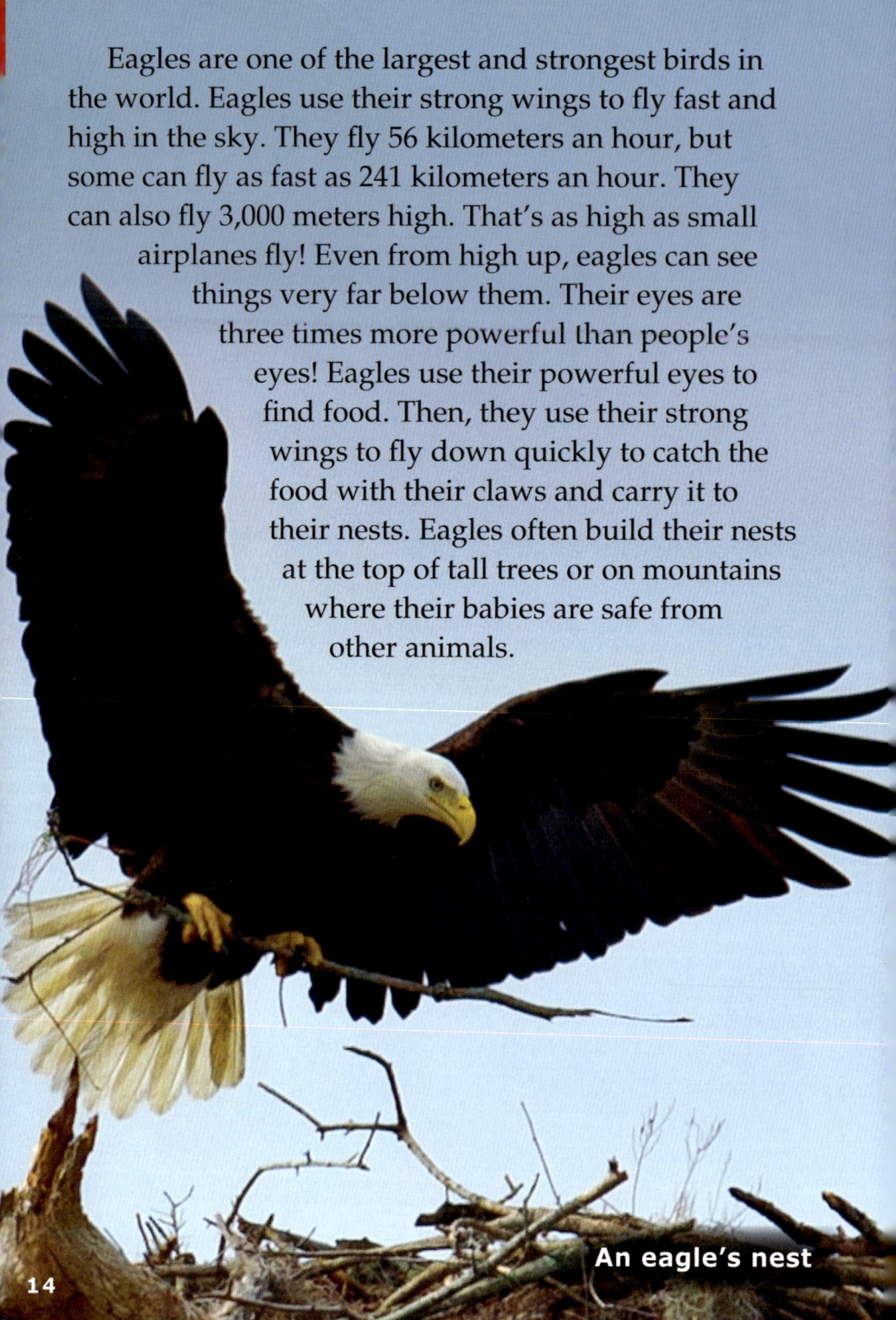

Eagles are one of the largest and strongest birds in the world. Eagles use their strong wings to fly fast and high in the sky. They fly 56 kilometers an hour, but some can fly as fast as 241 kilometers an hour. They can also fly 3,000 meters high. That's as high as small airplanes fly! Even from high up, eagles can see things very far below them. Their eyes are three times more powerful than people's eyes! Eagles use their powerful eyes to find food. Then, they use their strong wings to fly down quickly to catch the food with their claws and carry it to their nests. Eagles often build their nests at the top of tall trees or on mountains where their babies are safe from other animals.

An eagle's nest

Look at the flying fish in the picture. Are those wings? No, they are fins. Flying fish can stay in the air for 45 seconds and fly 50 meters with those fins! Flying fish got their name because they look like they are flying. They do not jump out of the water to find food. They jump out of the water to be safe from danger.

Animals' arms can be called different things: arms, flippers, wings, or fins. Even though they have different names, they all help the animals move in special and important ways.

? ANALYZE

What other animals do you know that have flippers or wings?

CHAPTER 4

Escape!

THERE ARE SOME ANIMALS THAT DO NOT USE ARMS OR LEGS TO MOVE. THEY MOVE THEIR WHOLE BODIES INSTEAD. THE IMPORTANT THING IS TO MOVE FAST TO ESCAPE FROM DANGER.

A snake moves by lifting, or moving up, its body one part at a time. The first part lifts up, moves to the front, and comes down. Then the middle part lifts up, moves to the front, and comes down, too. Finally, the snake does the same thing with the end of its body. This kind of locomotion is called **slithering**. Snakes can slither very fast to catch food or **escape** from danger. The fastest snake, the Black Mamba, can slither about five meters in one second!

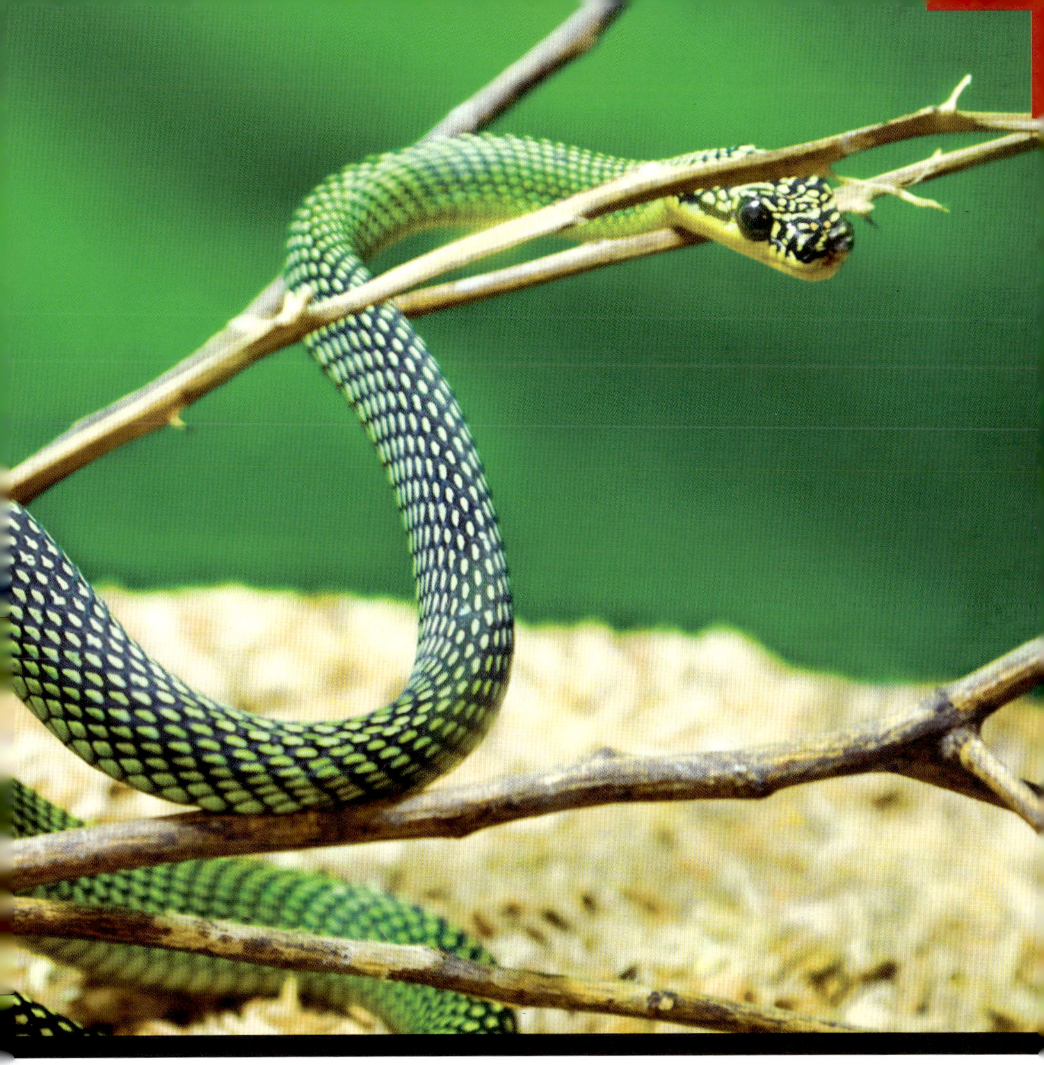

Video Quest

Sidewinders

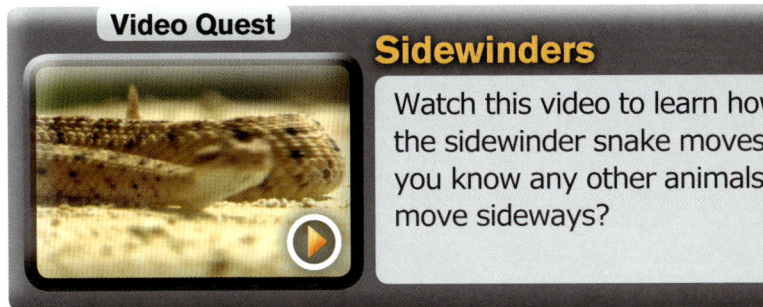

Watch this video to learn how the sidewinder snake moves. Do you know any other animals that move sideways?

Pangolins live in Africa and Asia. They have four legs, but when there is great danger, pangolins do not use their legs to run away. Instead, they roll into a ball. They make a circle with their bodies and put their heads under their tails. In that position,[4] pangolins can roll away from danger to escape from lions and other animals that want to eat them. But pangolins do not always have to roll away to be safe. Their bodies are very hard, so even lions with their sharp teeth and claws cannot eat pangolins when they roll into a ball. That's why pangolins always roll into a ball before they go to sleep.

A pangolin rolled into a ball.

Do flying squirrels really fly? Well, not really. They glide. Flying squirrels do not have wings like birds, but their arms and legs can work in a similar way. First, flying squirrels jump from trees. Then they put out their arms and legs. The wind catches the skin between their arms and legs and pushes them through the air. They use their tails to change direction[5] as they glide.

---

[4]**position:** the way someone or something is sitting, standing, or lying
[5]**direction:** the way someone or something is going

A flying squirrel

Flying squirrels can travel more than 30 meters in the air. This helps them escape danger quickly and be safe.

How do dolphins escape from danger? They swim, of course! But how? Dolphins use their tails to go faster and their fins to change direction. They usually travel five to eight kilometers an hour, but if they hurry, they can go as fast as 32 kilometers an hour. Dolphins move quickly in the water not only to be safe from danger. They also move quickly to catch their breakfast, lunch, and dinner.

Animals use many different kinds of locomotion. They might run, fly, swim, glide, slither, or even roll into a ball! Each animal uses its body the best way it can to stay safe.

? ANALYZE

An animal that moves too slowly can easily be killed. For example, a fast lion can catch a slow ostrich. Are there other reasons why an animal needs to move fast? How many can you think of?

CHAPTER 5

What Do You Think?

A hang glider

Do you remember all the different animals you read about and their kinds of locomotion? There are animals that run on four legs like horses, or on two legs like ostriches. Kangaroos hop on two legs, while grasshoppers hop on six. Centipedes walk on many, many legs!

There are animals that use their arms to move in important ways. Koalas and monkeys climb trees with their arms. Monkeys also use their arms to swing in trees. Penguins swim with their flippers, and eagles fly with their wings.

You also learned about animals that use their whole bodies to move. Snakes slither. Pangolins roll into a ball. Flying squirrels glide in the air. And dolphins swim in the sea.

People study the locomotion of animals and use the information in interesting ways. For example, people put flippers on their feet to swim more quickly. Airplanes and hang gliders have wings just like birds. After studying dolphins, people built submarines to move quickly in the ocean and stay under the water for a long time.

Look at the pictures on this page. What kind of locomotion do you see? What animals do they make you think of? Can you think of other ways people have learned from the locomotion of animals?

A pogo stick

Monkey bars

After You Read

Choose Ⓐ (True) or Ⓑ (False). If there isn't enough information in the book or videos to answer, choose Ⓒ (Doesn't say).

1 If a horse breaks its leg, the leg gets better quickly.

  Ⓐ True
  Ⓑ False
  Ⓒ Doesn't say

Video

2 The orangutan needs to use its whole hand when it swings between branches.

  Ⓐ True
  Ⓑ False
  Ⓒ Doesn't say

3 A grasshopper is an insect that has six legs.

  Ⓐ True
  Ⓑ False
  Ⓒ Doesn't say

4 *Centipede* is a word that means 1,000 feet.

  Ⓐ True
  Ⓑ False
  Ⓒ Doesn't say

5 Flying fish have bigger wings than eagles.

  Ⓐ True
  Ⓑ False
  Ⓒ Doesn't say

6 The pangolin sleeps in a ball.

  Ⓐ True
  Ⓑ False
  Ⓒ Doesn't say

Use the words in the box to complete the sentences.

climbs	flies	glides	hops	rolls	slithers

1 A snake _____ .

2 A pangolin _____ .

3 A koala _____ .

4 An eagle _____ .

5 A kangaroo _____ .

6 A flying squirrel _____ .

Complete the Chart

Can you move like these animals? Check (√) *Yes, I can* or *No, I can't*. For *No, I can't*, explain why you can't.

Animal	Yes, I can.	No, I can't. (explain why)
snake		
pangolin		
koala		
eagle		
kangaroo		
flying squirrel		

Answer Key

Words to Know, page 4

1 C **2** E **3** A **4** B **5** D

Words to Know, page 5

1 fins **2** tail **3** wings **4** claws **5** flippers

Analyze, page 5

Suggested Answer: They are the same because birds move their wings and fish move their fins in the same way. They are different because birds fly in the sky and fish swim in the water, and water is more difficult to move than air.

Analyze, page 7 *Answers will vary.*

Analyze, page 9 *Answers will vary.*

Video Quest, page 11

The gray kangaroo. Their big feet help kangaroos to hop fast. They don't become very tired when they hop fast.

Video Quest, page 13

Orangutans can hold a branch with just one finger.

Analyze, page 15 *Answers will vary.*

Video Quest, page 17 *Answers will vary.*

Analyze, page 19 *Answers will vary.*

True or False, page 22

1 B **2** B **3** A **4** B **5** C **6** A

Write, page 23

1 slithers **2** rolls **3** climbs **4** flies **5** hops **6** glides

Complete the Chart, page 23 *Answers will vary.*